SKYDIVING

SKYDIVING

ODYSSEYS

JIM WHITING

CREATIVE EDUCATION · CREATIVE PAPERBACKS

Published by Creative Education and Creative Paperbacks
P.O. Box 227, Mankato, Minnesota 56002
Creative Education and Creative Paperbacks
are imprints of The Creative Company
www.thecreativecompany.us

Design by Blue Design (www.bluedes.com)
Production by Joe Kahnke
Art direction by Rita Marshall
Printed in China

Photographs by Alamy (F1online digitale Bildagentur GmbH, mauritius images GmbH, Photo 12, Sueddeutsche Zeitung Photo, Joe Vogan, Gary Wainwright, ZUMA Press Inc), Charlotte Magazine (US Army Parachute Team), Creative Commons Wikimedia (B.Z. Berlin/Ratzer), Flickr (Tim Rothon Photography), Getty Images (Gary Connery Archive/Getty Images News, Norman Kent/Barcroft Media, LEON NEAL/AFP), iStockphoto (anilakduygu, German-skydiver), National Geographic Creative (Keith Ladzinski), Shutterstock (Flavio Almeida, Germanskydiver, Rick Neves, vivooo), Smithsonian Institution (National Air and Space Museum Archives)

Library of Congress Cataloging-in-Publication Data
Names: Whiting, Jim, author.
Title: Skydiving / Jim Whiting.
Series: Odysseys in extreme sports.
Includes bibliographical references and index.
Summary: An in-depth survey of the popular extreme sport of skydiving, from Leonardo da Vinci's sketches to the parachute-free wingsuit, as well as its records, equipment, and famous divers.
Identifiers: LCCN 2017028050 / ISBN 978-1-60818-695-2 (hardcover) / ISBN 978-1-62832-291-0 (pbk) / ISBN 978-1-56660-731-5 (eBook)

Subjects: LCSH: 1. Skydiving—Juvenile literature.
Classification: LCC GV770 .W48 2018 / DDC 797.5/6—dc23

CCSS: RI 8.1, 2, 3, 4, 5, 8, 10; RI 9-10.1, 2, 3, 4, 5, 8, 10; RI 11-12.1, 2, 3, 4, 5, 10; RST 6-8.1, 2, 5, 6, 10; RST 9-10.1, 2, 5, 6, 10; RST 11-12.1, 2, 5, 6, 10

First Edition HC 9 8 7 6 5 4 3 2 1
First Edition PBK 9 8 7 6 5 4 3 2 1

CONTENTS

Introduction

Soured on soccer? Fed up with football? Bored by baseball? Turned off by team sports? If so, extreme sports might be more to your liking. While there's not an exact definition of what makes a sport "extreme," the following characteristics (or at least most of them) seem to be common: a higher degree of risk despite use of protective gear, emphasis on achieving high speeds and/or

OPPOSITE: Skydivers commonly jump from an altitude of 13,000 feet (3,962 m), and many wear helmets with mounted cameras so that they can relive their experience and share it with others.

heights, more likely to be performed alone or with a handful of friends, no issues with playing time as in team sports, stunts requiring substantial amounts of skill and practice, less emphasis on formal rules, and an **adrenaline** rush from physical exertion.

It's hard to find a sport more extreme than skydiving. You're standing in the doorway of an airplane, looking at the ground three miles (4.8 km) below. You take a deep breath and jump. Within seconds, you're falling at speeds faster than 100 miles (161 km) per hour. If you're feeling especially brave, you perform rolls, turns, or even backflips before pulling the **ripcord** on your parachute. Soon you're only a few feet above the ground. You make one final turn into the wind and step onto the solid earth, as easily as getting out of a car. You've just completed a skydive!

What Goes Up Must Come Down—Safely

Historians believe Italian inventor and artist Leonardo da Vinci was the first to dream up a parachute, in about 1495. In one of his notebooks is a drawing of a man clutching ropes connected to the corners of a pyramid-shaped frame covered by cloth. About a century later, Fausto Veranzio constructed a device similar to da Vinci's

Testing da Vinci

British skydiver Adrian Nichols wanted to prove that Leonardo da Vinci's parachute design would work. Nichols's model weighed nearly 200 pounds (90.7 kg) and was made of canvas, wooden poles, and ropes. In May 2000, he strapped himself into the parachute, which was connected to a hot-air balloon. He rose to 10,000 feet (3,048 m), and then released the parachute from the balloon. His five-minute descent was slow and comfortable. Nichols was afraid the parachute's weight would crush him if he rode it all the way down. So he released himself at 2,000 feet (610 m) and used his reserve parachute to land. "It took one of the greatest minds who ever lived to design it, but it took 500 years to find a man with a brain small enough to actually go and fly it," he joked.

concept, leaped from the bell tower of St. Mark's Cathedral in Venice, and landed unhurt.

In the late 1700s, French brothers Joseph-Michel and Jacques-Étienne Montgolfier built a hot-air balloon, which carried people higher than ever before. The brothers experimented with attaching animals to primitive parachutes and dropping them from the balloon. Jean-Pierre Blanchard, who worked with the Montgolfiers, coined the word "parachute." It comes from two French words: *para*, which means "defense against," and *chute*, which means "a fall." In 1797, An-

OPPOSITE During the early days of parachuting, Käthe Paulus completed more than 165 jumps from hot-air balloons and performed aerial acrobatics under the stage name Miss Polly.

dré-Jacques Garnerin used a parachute when he jumped from a height of more than 2,000 feet (610 m) above Paris, France. Five years later, he leaped from a balloon 8,000 feet (2,438 m) above London, England. To ease the severe **oscillations** that threatened his safety at such heights, he cut a small hole in the top of the parachute. The vent enabled a smoother descent.

Advances during the next century improved the safety and reliability of parachutes. Some people began using them for circus acts. Women also began making public parachute jumps. Around 1900, Käthe Paulus became the first German woman to parachute from a hot-air balloon. She was also credited with inventing the folding (knapsack) parachute. In 1913, Georgia "Tiny" Broadwick became the first woman to parachute from an airplane.

The recently invented airplane opened up new possibilities for parachutists. Daredevils thrilled onlookers by jumping from airplanes several thousand feet above the earth, and then falling gracefully to the ground.

During World War I (1914–18), both sides lofted lighter-than-air balloons near the front lines to observe enemy **emplacements**. These balloons were prime targets for enemy aircraft to attack. Balloon crews were provided with parachutes to enable them to escape, but airplane pilots were forbidden to carry parachutes. Commanders thought that timid pilots would jump to safety rather than engage in combat.

The frames of these early airplanes were wooden and covered with fabric that was sealed and stiffened with flammable glue. The planes themselves were powered by gas engines. Enemy bullets often ignited fires, which the **slipstream** quickly blew back into the cockpit. Flying far too high to land immediately, pilots frequently faced the horrible choice of being burned alive or hurling themselves out of the inferno and falling thousands of feet to their deaths. Military leaders changed their minds after the war ended and allowed pilots to wear parachutes. But that decision was too late for hundreds of pilots who had perished because they couldn't "bail out" of doomed aircraft.

Soon after the war ended, there was a big jump in barnstorming. **Troupes** of traveling aviators would perform daredevil stunts. One of the biggest crowd pleasers was the "low-pull" contest. Two or more people (almost always men) would jump from an airplane at the same time. They would play a game of chicken on their way down, waiting to see who would inflate his parachute first. Occasionally, the "winner" would wait too long and thud into the ground, his parachute only partly open.

The first formal parachute competitions began in the Soviet Union in 1930. Two years later the United States held its first event. The object was to land as close as possible to a predetermined target.

Much more ominously, a **resurgent** German military pioneered the development of parachuting soldiers during this era. These troops were known as *fallschirmjäger*, or "tumbling umbrella hunters," and they achieved notable successes during the early days of World War II (1939–45). The British and Americans soon began training and deploying their own airborne soldiers. Thousands of these American and British paratroopers famously landed behind enemy lines in the middle of the night before the D-Day invasion of Normandy, France on

German Paratroopers

German paratroopers played a key role in the early months of World War II. In May 1940, fewer than 100 German parachutists launched a surprise attack on a key fort in Belgium, killing or capturing more than 1,000 Belgian soldiers. Other parachutists seized three vital bridges. Their efforts helped German ground troops quickly conquer Belgium. The paratroopers had similar success in neighboring Holland. A year later, they parachuted onto the Greek island of Crete. This time, however, the defenders had advance warning. Though the *fallschirmjäger* emerged victorious, they suffered such heavy losses that German dictator Adolf Hitler refused to allow further large-scale airborne attacks. Still, the *fallschirmjäger* were among Germany's best soldiers. Allied forces called them "green devils."

June 6, 1944. And unlike in World War I, plane crews in the Second World War were routinely provided with parachutes. Tens of thousands of aviators escaped from doomed aircraft by "hitting the silk."

Following the war, British and American paratroopers relished the opportunity to jump without being shot at. As the British Parachute Association notes, "There were plenty of surplus parachutes and it was at that time when the then current and former military parachutists began to enjoy and exploit the potential of parachuting as a sport." Many people on the ground watched them and wanted to try parachute jumping for themselves. The term "skydive" originated during the 1950s, and the first skydiving schools opened in 1957. The Parachute Club of America was formed about this time, becoming known as the U.S. Parachute Association (USPA) in 1967.

As more people began skydiving, they wanted chutes that were easier to control than those used by the military. Military parachutes—still in use today for dropping cargo and other purposes—were reliable and opened easily. But jumpers were at the mercy of the wind, sometimes winding up far from their intended target on the ground.

That control came with a radical redesign of the parachute in the 1960s. What became known as the ram-air parafoil would revolutionize the fledgling sport. Unlike dome-shaped conventional parachutes, the ram-air para-

BELOW In formation skydiving competitions, groups of 4, 8, or 16—plus a videographer—must complete their formations within a specified time. They are judged based on the video recorded in the air.

foil is rectangular and operates more like airplane wings. The forward motion of the chute "rams" air into vents at the leading edge of the chute and inflates a series of cells to create lift. Parachutists can control the direction of travel and rate of descent, allowing them to virtually pinpoint landings.

The new parafoil set the stage for the growth of interest in skydiving. People could now enjoy the exhilaration of **free fall**, and then deploy their parachutes and come down wherever they wanted. It didn't take long for skydivers to want to share the experience with others. Groups began leaping together and forming designs during free fall. At first, these designs were simple and involved only a handful of people. Today, hundreds of people may jump from multiple aircraft and form intricate patterns in the air.

Made up of 12 members, the Red Devils is the parachute display team of the British army. The group performs about 60 exhibition jumps each year in an effort to gain support and recruit for the military.

Gearing Up and Playing Games

Once someone decides to plunge into skydiving, the first task is to find a skydiving center, or drop zone. Most are located at small airports outside cities or in rural areas. Virtually all require that prospective skydivers are at least 18 years old, though a few accept 16- and 17-year-olds with written parental permission.

The most important piece of gear is the parachute itself, attached to the

OPPOSITE: In addition to a parachute, most skydivers wear a special jumpsuit, helmet, and goggles. Another important piece of gear is an altimeter watch, which shows distance from the ground.

jumper's body with a harness. While parachutes were made primarily of silk during the first decades of the 20th century, most today are **nylon**. Tucked in with the main chute is a pilot chute. When the ripcord is pulled, the pilot chute pops out and quickly inflates. That, in turn, pulls out the main chute, which ensures that it deploys in the proper shape. Skydivers also pack a reserve parachute, in the statistically unlikely but nevertheless very real possibility that the main chute fails.

Many, but not all, skydivers wear protective helmets. Goggles are vital for two reasons. First, they prevent blurry vision that would otherwise occur from the watering of the eyes from the onrushing air. Second, they keep out unwanted objects such as dust particles or bugs. Most divers also wear colorful one-piece jumpsuits. To gain more speed, these jumpsuits are often tight-fitting. If they are participating in some sort of formation, though, divers need something a little looser to give other divers something to grab.

Military paratroopers wear heavy boots, in part to protect their feet and legs from landing in unknown, harsh terrain but also because they often need to march long distances to engage their enemies. Sport divers, however, almost always land in well-groomed zones and don't need to worry about marching off. So they wear lightweight footwear such as running shoes.

TAKEAWAY

Tandem skydiving accounts for more than half of all first jumps. It is the easiest way to get started.

Some even go barefoot.

Those new to skydiving have three ways to get introduced to the sport. Tandem skydiving accounts for more than half of all first jumps. The student is harnessed to an instructor during the entire descent. It is the easiest way to get started, as there is just half an hour of basic instruction. Some prefer to go solo for their first attempt and may choose static-line or instructor-assisted deployment (IAD). Following several hours of ground instruction, the student goes aloft. The parachute is deployed by a static line attached to the aircraft or by an instructor as soon as the student begins the jump, so there is almost no free fall. The student receives continuous radio instruction during the descent to ensure a safe landing.

Many first-time skydivers opt for a tandem jump. The student wears a harness and is strapped onto the instructor, who wears the parachute and is responsible for making a safe landing.

Those who feel like jumping on their own the first time can also opt for Accelerated Free Fall (AFF). It begins with four or five hours of ground instruction, including basic body positioning and hand signals. When that's completed, students jump with two instructors, who hold onto the student's harness during free fall until it's time to pull the ripcord. Then the instructors provide radio advice until the student is safely on the ground.

Those who continue with the sport following their first jump will become more skillful at free fall. Experienced skydivers can attain speeds of up to 300 miles (483 km) per hour. However, it's more common for students' speeds to range between 110 and 130 miles (177–209 km) per hour. That means they descend about 175 feet (53.3 m) per second! Once the parachute opens, the speed slows dramatically. Films of skydivers make it seem as though the change is almost instantaneous, but that's mainly because the videographer continues free-falling. In reality, the slowdown is somewhat gradual.

Competitive skydiving takes several forms. One is style. The contestant goes through a series of predetermined maneuvers, such as backflips and turns. Another is accuracy. As the diver lands, he or she must touch down inside a target, which can be as small as 15 inches (38.1 cm) in diameter. The best skydivers hit a tiny yellow dot in the center of the circle.

OPPOSITE Advancements in skydiving equipment have given divers greater control, allowing them to guide their parachutes to a precise landing spot.

A third, much less common, form of competition is the number of jumps in a 24-hour period. It is an intricate procedure, often requiring more than 100 volunteers. Typically, a skydiver will use 3 or 4 planes flying in relays and up to 25 parachutes. As soon as the diver lands—as close as possible to a waiting aircraft—several volunteers help him or her unbuckle the parachute. Other volunteers help the diver buckle into another parachute before he or she dashes to the waiting aircraft. Under ideal circumstances, this part of the process takes less than 10 seconds.

The plane takes off immediately and flies to an altitude of about 2,000 feet (610 m). During the steep ascent, which takes about a minute, a jumpmaster keeps the diver from rolling out. As the plane levels off, he checks out the gear while the diver gulps down **electrolyte**-filled beverages. Because airplane engines constantly generate poisonous carbon monoxide gas, the diver may also need to take some breaths from an oxygen tank.

By then, the aircraft has reached the drop point. The skydiver jumps out, immediately deploys the parachute, and lands about 45 seconds later. The process is repeated as many times as possible. The current record is 640 jumps, set in 2006 in Indiana by Jay Stokes, a former Green Beret. It was the fifth time that Stokes established the record. He recorded 331 jumps on his first try, in 1995. Then came 384 (1997), 476 (1999), and 534 (2003). In September 2014, Stokes hoped to do 700 jumps in a single day to raise money for charity. He spent nearly a year preparing for the event. Unfortunately, the one element he couldn't control—the weather—sabotaged his effort.

The failure didn't harm Stokes's standing in the skydiving community, though. "Right now, in world records for the most jumps in 24 hours, Jay's so far ahead of everyone else that there really isn't anyone who even wants to try to compete with him," notes his website.

BASE Jumping

Every October, nearly 400 people jump off the New River Bridge near Fayetteville, West Virginia and float 876 feet (267 m) to the bottom as part of the city's annual Bridge Day. It's the world's largest group BASE jump. A BASE jump is a parachute jump from any fixed object that rises high into the air. BASE stands for (B)uildings, (A)ntennas, S(pans), and E(arth, or cliffs). The term was invented in 1981 by Carl Boenish, a filmmaker who specialized in recording these events and set a world record in 1984 for the highest BASE jump at 3,600 feet (1,097 m). BASE jumping can be very dangerous. The altitude is much lower than jumping from an airplane, so there's little room for error. Open the chute too early and you run the risk of hitting the object. Too late and you could be killed.

Famous Skydivers

With parachuting becoming so popular around the turn of the 20th century, it is no wonder that a teenaged single mom named Georgia Ann Thompson was fascinated by a performance from a group named "The Broadwicks and Their Famous French Aeronauts" at the 1907 North Carolina State Fair. Troupe members ascended several thousand feet in hot-air balloons, and then parachuted back to the earth.

Georgia Ann worked 14-hour days in cotton mills to help support her family. She pleaded with show owner Charles Broadwick to let her join the troupe instead. Leaving her daughter with her mother, Georgia went with Broadwick. According to some accounts, he legally adopted her to avoid the scandal of a young girl traveling with an older man.

Now known as Tiny Broadwick, she became one of the show's top performers because of her small size (she was less than 5 feet [1.5 m] tall and weighed about 85 pounds [38.6 kg]) and willingness to do dangerous stunts. "I was never afraid," she said. "I'd go up any time, any place. The only thing I hated was getting back to Earth so quickly."

Balloon jumping lost its popularity with the rise of

OPPOSITE Fearless Tiny Broadwick served as an adviser to the U.S. Army Air Corps during World War I. In World War II, she visited military bases and convinced soldiers that if she could survive a jump, they could, too.

dependable aircraft. Pioneering pilot Glenn Martin asked Tiny to leave Broadwick and work for him. Broadwick approved, and even made a special parachute for her. In 1913, Tiny became the first woman to parachute from an airplane. She was also the first woman to deliberately parachute into water. And she was the first person—male or female—to make a planned free fall. She made more than 1,100 jumps before retiring in 1922.

Half a century later, Cheryl Stearns began her own brilliant career as a skydiver. When she was 17, she

OPPOSITE With more than 20,000 jumps to her credit, Cheryl Stearns has made landings in 35 countries, touching down in such spots as the Statue of Liberty, a pool at SeaWorld, and underneath the Gateway Arch.

talked her mom into letting her take skydiving lessons. Her dad offered to pay for flying lessons instead. But Cheryl did both, becoming perhaps the greatest-ever female skydiver and also a commercial pilot.

It didn't take long for her to make her mark as a skydiver. In 1978, at the age of 24, she became the Women's Overall World Champion in style and accuracy parachuting. She won her second title 16 years later. Stearns had joined the U.S. Army in 1977. Soon she became the first female member of the Golden Knights, the army's precision demonstration parachute team. She was especially noted for carrying the American flag to a landing at the base of the Statue of Liberty.

Eventually, Stearns went on to compile 30 world records. She has made more than 20,000 jumps, by far the largest total for any woman. She also set the standard

for women in jumps during a 24-hour period, with 352 in 1995. More than half of those dives ended with her landing on a 2-inch (5.1 cm) target—including 84 times at night.

Stearns continues to maintain her elite status in competition. In 2014, at the age of 60, she helped her team win first place in Team Accuracy at the U.S. National Skydiving Championships. She also captured first place in several individual women's categories. To give back to the sport, Stearns runs an annual style and accuracy training camp in Lodi, California.

A common joke is that everyone gets 15 minutes of fame. For Google engineer Alan Eustace, those 15 minutes came on October 24, 2014. Eustace—then 57 years old—set world records for the highest altitude from which a jump began (135,890 feet [41,419 m]) and longest free fall (15 minutes). "There is an incredible amount of risk," said former astronaut Mark Kelly, who witnessed the event. "To do it safely is a testament to the people involved."

Eustace began his flight from an abandoned airport in Roswell, New Mexico. He wore a custom-built spacesuit with a specially developed life-support system. A balloon filled with helium carried him more than 25 miles (40.2 km) above the earth. The ascent lasted more than two hours. Eustace had to remain as still as possible to avoid overheating from the direct rays of the sun.

When he reached the maximum altitude, he fired a small explosive charge to release himself from the balloon. His top speed during descent was more than 800 miles (1,287 km) per hour. That set off a **sonic boom** that people on the ground heard, though Eustace said he didn't hear or feel it. "It was a wild, wild ride," he said of his descent. "It was amazing. It was beautiful. You could see the darkness of space and you could see the layers of atmosphere, which I had never seen before."

Although few people knew his name, Mark Sutton achieved his 15 minutes of fame at the Opening Ceremonies of the 2012 Summer Olympic Games in London, England. Preparations for the "moment" began several months earlier and were top-secret. Actor Daniel Craig, playing the role of famed secret agent James Bond, was filmed escorting Queen Elizabeth II to a waiting helicopter. Then the two flew to the site of the Olympic Stadium.

On the night of the opening ceremonies, spectators watched the footage on giant TV monitors in the Olympic Stadium. Moments later, a helicopter like the one in the video flew overhead. To the delight and astonishment of the onlookers, "Craig" and "the queen" leaped out and skydived to the ground. Acting as stunt doubles were Sutton in a tuxedo and his friend and fellow skydiver Gary Connery in a wig and a

Professional stuntman Gary Connery (left) has performed midair feats for many films, including *Batman Begins* and *Harry Potter and the Chamber of Secrets*. In 2012, he teamed up with Mark Sutton (right) to perform stunts for the opening act of the Summer Olympics.

TONY
SUIT
GoPro

pink dress. Soon afterward, the real queen appeared in the stadium and took part in the official opening. Movie director Danny Boyle, who was in charge of the Opening Ceremonies, said that Sutton and Connery "made the stadium gasp ... and left indelible memories for people from all walks of life all over the world." As a result of their leap, Sutton and Connery were briefly the world's most famous skydivers.

In addition to his obvious skills as a skydiver, Sutton was regarded as one of the top wingsuit flyers in the world. Sadly, he died in 2013, as the result of a wingsuit flying accident in Switzerland.

Diving into Culture

In the past few decades, skydiving has become an important part of popular culture. Its hints of danger and spectacular stunts have made it irresistible to authors, filmmakers, video game designers, and many others.

Noted young people's author Gary Paulsen brought his trademark realism to skydiving in 1999 in *World of Adventure: Skydive!* The main character, 13-year-old Jesse

Rodriguez, helps out his friend Buck, who owns a small airport and skydiving school. Jesse is counting the days until he can make his first jump. Conflict arises when Jesse discovers that a Central American drug **cartel** is using the airport to smuggle its members into the U.S. Even worse, Buck might be involved in this operation. This knowledge puts Jesse and his friend Robin in danger. They make their first jumps a lot earlier than they had planned and under very different circumstances.

Author Bill Myers has a series of books about so-called super-nerd Wally McDoogle. In *My Life as a Screaming Skydiver* (1998), Wally and his two best friends, Wall Street and Opera, are playing laser tag when they learn about the mysterious—and deadly—Giggle Gun. Aided by British secret service agent James Blond, they must find the Giggle Gun before the bad guys do. Eventually,

Wally has to make a desperate parachute leap from a fast-moving jet plane to achieve their goal.

Movie producers have long realized that audiences love skydiving scenes. Many James Bond films feature skydiving sequences. B. J. Worth's credentials as a world-champion skydiver prompted the producers of the 1979 Bond film *Moonraker* to hire him to coordinate the movie's memorable parachute scene. It begins with Bond (played by Roger Moore), pushing a man wearing a parachute out of a plane after a fistfight.

Moments later, Bond himself is pushed out—without a parachute. After a long free fall, he catches up with the bad guy. They struggle and Bond takes the parachute away, leaving his foe to plummet to the earth. Yet another danger remains for Bond: a steel-toothed character named Jaws (Richard Kiel) has followed him down. The entire sequence, which lasts barely a minute and a half on-screen, required 80 separate jumps to complete.

The producers were so impressed with Worth's work that they hired him for subsequent Bond films. As *People* magazine notes, "Worth dreamed up the jump from Paris's Eiffel Tower that opened *A View to a Kill* [1985], and for a fee of $30,000 agreed to perform the dangerous stunt. Stunt-doubling for [actress] Grace Jones, he launched himself with a running start from a tiny platform on the observation deck 900 feet [274 m] from the ground while three high-speed cameras rolled to shoot the scene in slow motion. After a three-second free fall, Worth pulled his ripcord and floated down to within six feet [1.8 m] of his wife, Bobbie … and their daughter, Sara."

A number of other films are either centered on skydiving or make it an important part of the action. In 1969's *Gypsy Moths*, Burt Lancaster, Gene Hackman, and Scott Wilson star as skydivers who travel around the country and put on shows. Even though skydiving was still in its infancy then, the three men provided a glimpse of the future by performing in wingsuits. Director John Frankenheimer called it his favorite film and was disappointed that it wasn't widely shown in the U.S. It did much better in Australia and helped popularize skydiving there.

THE ONLY LAW
THAT MATTERS
IS GRAVITY
POINT
BREAK
DMG
THIS CHRISTMAS
SEE IT IN REAL D 3D

OPPOSITE Several films have increased public awareness of and interest in skydiving by showcasing thrilling sequences of sky-high acrobatics.

In *Point Break* (1991), FBI agent Johnny Utah (played by Keanu Reeves) joins a gang of surfers he thinks are behind a string of bank robberies. At one point, the leader, Bodhi (Patrick Swayze), takes Utah skydiving. In a later scene, Utah free-falls after Bodhi, who manages to make his escape. Some skydivers complained that the movie showed unrealistically long conversations during free fall. But moviegoers responded by turning up in droves to try skydiving.

U.S. Marshal Pete Nessip (played by Wesley Snipes) is escorting a prisoner in an airplane in *Drop Zone* (1994). The prisoner, a computer hacker, escapes by parachuting from the plane. Nessip believes a skydiver formerly with the Drug Enforcement Agency (DEA) named Ty Moncrief (Gary Busey) masterminded the escape, so he learns how to dive. Eventually Nessip discovers Moncrief's plot to parachute onto DEA headquarters so the hacker can gain access to the mainframe computer and sell the names of federal agents to drug cartels. Aided by his skydiving teacher, Nessip seeks to thwart the plan.

Starring Jack Nicholson and Morgan Freeman, *The Bucket List* (2007) introduced millions more viewers to the sport. Skydiving is on a list of things the two men want to do before "kicking the bucket" (dying). The film opens with a skydiving scene. Each man is linked to an instructor. During the free fall, Nicholson exults, "How about this, huh? This is really living!" Freeman, who from the start of the scene has been terrified, replies, "I hate your rotten guts!"

A number of video games include skydiving as part of the action. For example, it was introduced in *Grand Theft Auto: San Andreas* (2004), and made a reappearance in

Grand Theft Auto: V (2013) when a character is required to undergo aviation training to complete a mission. The *Saints Row* series also includes skydiving action.

For less violent plots and more focus on the sport of skydiving, there are games like *Base Jumping* (2007) and *Go! Sports—Skydiving* (2008). For a taste of wingsuit flying, check out *Skydive: Proximity Flight* (2013). Developers worked closely with several noted BASE jumpers to ensure the effects were as realistic as possible.

The Future

With skydiving firmly entrenched in the popular imagination, many people are turning their thoughts to the future of the sport. Perhaps the most obvious trend is indoor skydiving, which takes place in a vertical wind tunnel. Inside the structure, air blows upward at a speed of about 120 miles (193 km) per hour, the **terminal velocity** of a falling human body. It gives you the sensation of floating because the rising air cancels

---

OPPOSITE: A diver who jumps from an altitude of 13,000 feet (3,962 m) will spend roughly 50 seconds in free fall, followed by a 4- to 5-minute parachute ride to the ground.

out the effects of gravity. The first vertical wind tunnel was built in the 1960s at Wright-Patterson Air Force Base in Ohio. The first one constructed for commercial purposes opened in Las Vegas, Nevada, in 1982. The concept received widespread exposure during the closing ceremonies at the 2006 Winter Olympics in Turin, Italy. Skydivers soared as high as 50 feet (15.2 m) above a specially designed vertical wind tunnel.

While it can't duplicate the experience of seeing Earth from three miles (4.8 km) up before free-falling, indoor skydiving does have several advantages. It eliminates anxiety for people with a fear of heights or jumping from an airplane. They hover just a few feet above a trampoline-style netting. Second, there's almost no limit to the amount of free fall that participants can experience. This is especially attractive to competitive

Four-Legged Leapers

The military employs skydiving dogs. Their use began during World War II, when the animals and their handlers parachuted into remote areas that would have been impossible to reach by land. The dogs searched for booby traps, carried supplies, detected enemy troops, and located victims of plane crashes and helped bring them to safety. More recently, U.S. Special Forces have used skydiving dogs in the Middle East. The dogs are securely attached to their human handlers as they jump. They sniff out hidden bombs after they land. The dogs' keen sense of smell can also give their human companions advance notice of enemy forces lying in ambush. Civilians sometimes jump with their pets. A pug named Otis has made more than 60 jumps, wearing “doggles” to protect his eyes.

OPPOSITE Indoor skydiving facilities give people the chance to experience the sensation of flying without having to jump from an airplane.

skydivers, who can practice their maneuvers over and over until they feel confident. Third, there is no minimum age. Children as young as three can take part in indoor skydiving.

Participants begin with a safety and technique briefing. Then they put on a jumpsuit, helmet, and goggles. When they enter the wind tunnel, they simply lean forward and the uprushing air makes them immediately airborne. An instructor is always nearby. Because of the noise of the air, the instructor uses hand signals rather than trying to shout.

The number of indoor skydiving facilities appears to be steadily increasing. Royal Caribbean International's *Quantum of the Seas* boasted the first-ever seaborne skydiving facility when it launched in 2014. Mounted near the stern of the ship, the 23-foot (7 m) device provides

BODYFLIGHT.CO.UK

ROZLUŹNIJ SIĘ
RELAX
OK.KEEP GOING
SPOT

Indoor wind tunnels have made the sport available to a wider group of people, including children as young as three years old. More experienced divers can use the tunnels to safely practice their skills closer to the ground.

passengers with a superb view in addition to the thrill of the sensation of skydiving.

Skydivers are always experimenting with new ways to make their sport more fun and more challenging. One recent example is skysurfing. Skysurfers ride a special board that closely resembles a snowboard, with bindings that can be released in the event of an emergency. During free fall, they do tricks such as spins, flips, and especially the helicopter—turning their bodies so the board is uppermost and spinning. The motion resembles the descent of a maple tree seed or a helicopter's rotor blades. A person with a head-mounted camera usually accompanies skysurfers, capturing the action before they pull their ripcords.

A developing trend in the sport would do away with parachutes altogether. Solar System Express is designing what the company calls a space diving suit. Space divers would be taken high into the stratosphere, and then free-fall back to the surface. Instead of deploying a parachute to achieve a soft landing, tiny rocket booster engines mounted in **gyroscopic** boots would slow the space diver, orient him properly, and allow him to make a soft, two-footed landing. An interactive screen in the helmet would provide continuous displays of critical information such as altitude and speed.

Another no-more-parachute trend is in wingflying. Wingflyers are hoping to realize a dream as old as the ancient Greek myth of Daedalus and Icarus: to fly. Though still highly dangerous, the takeoff and flight of

Flying Like a Bird

Some skydivers have found a way of making their free fall last longer. It's called wingsuit flying. Wingsuiters wear an outfit that makes them look a little like flying squirrels. Two layers of extra fabric extend from their wrists to their hips and between their legs. As soon as they exit an aircraft, they spread their arms and legs as widely as possible. Air rushes inside between the two layers, which helps create lift. Typically, wingsuiters fall only half as fast as skydivers, while achieving horizontal speeds that are up to three times faster. When they get close to the ground, they deploy a parachute to land safely. Wingsuit flying is definitely not for beginners. Experts recommend making at least 500 skydives before trying out a wingsuit.

wingflyers have become relatively routine. The challenge, as gymnasts might say, is to "stick the landing." The key to doing that is to reduce the vertical speed by tweaking the design of the suit so that the diver can glide to a soft, comfortable landing without needing a parachute. One way to accomplish this is to ease down into deep snow on the side of a mountain. On May 20, 2012, Gary Connery landed in a huge pile of cardboard boxes without using his parachute. He emerged without any ill effects.

Like any other sport—extreme or otherwise—that keeps records, skydivers are likely to continue challenging those marks as they push the boundaries of what is possible. For example, Pat Moorehead celebrated his 80th birthday in 2011 by making 80 skydives in a single day—a world record for his age group. The feat took about six and a half hours, and Moorehead actually made an 81st

OPPOSITE One hundred divers from all around the world jumped from 5 different airplanes and joined together in diamond formation to complete the 100 Way Canopy world record in 2007.

jump to descend with an American flag.

Moorehead was also part of another world record the following year. Sixty members of Skydivers Over Sixty linked up in a formation during a 90-second free fall over Lake Elsinore, California, becoming the largest-ever group in that age category. Participants came from as far away as Australia, Germany, and Italy. "You don't stop skydiving because you get old," Moorehead said. "You've got to keep moving." These will likely prove to be words to live by for other skydivers as they age, and it's possible that someone will set out to break Moorehead's record.

Also in 2012, 138 people set a new record for the most skydivers in a vertical formation, which meant they were pointed straight down. Organizer Rook Nelson explained that it is "basically doing a headstand" in midair, allowing the divers to achieve speeds of nearly 200 miles (322

km) per hour and making the linking-up process more difficult—and more hazardous—than standard formation flying. "It's going to be like someone running a red light and you taking them out," he added, referring to risks the later arrivals face as they join the group. It took 15 attempts spread over a 3-day period to achieve the feat.

Skydivers wouldn't have it any other way. The element of risk is always there. But so are the rewards. And those are all the sweeter because of the thrill of being totally free as they plummet toward the earth.

Glossary

adrenaline a substance produced by the body, often when physically or emotionally stressed, characterized by increased blood flow and heightened excitement

cartel an association that seeks to maintain high prices of something by controlling its supply

electrolyte salts and minerals that control the body's electrical impulses and thereby maintain high levels of proper functioning

emplacements positions of military weapons and troop concentrations

free fall the period between the time skydivers leave an airplane and the deployment of their parachutes

gyroscopic related to a device that is mounted and able to spin quickly around an axis or midpoint

nylon a strong, lightweight, durable, and flexible artificial fabric

oscillations continual swings

resurgent reviving after a period of little activity

ripcord the handle attached to the parachute pack

slipstream a current of air generated by an airplane propeller

sonic boom the sound associated with the shock waves generated as an object traveling through the air surpasses the speed of sound

terminal velocity the highest speed of a falling object, when the downward pull of gravity equals the resistance of the air through which it is falling

troupes groups of entertainers who travel to different locations

Selected Bibliography

Buchanan, Tom. *Jump!: Skydiving Made Fun and Easy.* New York: McGraw-Hill, 2003.

Fortenberry, Dick. *No ETA: The Pioneering Days of Skydiving.* Bloomington, Ind.: iUniverse, 2011.

Hearn, Peter. *The Sky People: A History of Parachuting.* North Branch, Minn.: Specialty Press, 1997.

Higgins, Matt. *Bird Dream: Adventures at the Extremes of Human Flight.* New York: Penguin, 2014.

Hopkins, Ellen. *The Golden Knights: The U.S. Army Parachute Team.* North Mankato, Minn.: Capstone, 2001.

Lehne, Chris. *The Newbie's Guide to Skydiving.* Seattle: Amazon Digital Services, 2012.

Miller, John. *Skydiving for Beginners.* Seattle: Amazon Digital Services, 2012.

Poynter, Dan, and Mike Turoff. *Parachuting: The Skydiver's Handbook.* 10th ed. Santa Barbara, Calif.: Para, 2007.

Websites

Dropzone.com: Skydiving Community, Skydive Information

http://www.dropzone.com

This comprehensive site provides information for skydivers of all levels. It includes a directory and reviews of more than 1,200 outdoor and 55 indoor skydive centers worldwide, plus safety information, forums, a calendar of upcoming events, and more.

United States Parachute Association

http://www.uspa.org

The official website of USPA includes news and upcoming events, skydiving history and terminology, types of competition, ways to get started in the sport, Parachutist e-zine, and more.

Note: Every effort has been made to ensure that any websites listed above were active at the time of publication. However, because of the nature of the Internet, it is impossible to guarantee that these sites will remain active indefinitely or that their contents will not be altered.

Index